This book is to be retu~~~~~~~~

D0236334

2·99

THE VICTORIA AND ALBERT COLOUR BOOKS

FIRST PUBLISHED IN GREAT BRITAIN BY
WEBB & BOWER (PUBLISHERS) LIMITED
9 COLLETON CRESCENT, EXETER, DEVON EX2 4 BY
AND MICHAEL JOSEPH LIMITED, 27 WRIGHTS LANE, LONDON W8 5TZ
IN ASSOCIATION WITH THE VICTORIA AND ALBERT MUSEUM, LONDON

FIRST PUBLISHED 1987
SECOND IMPRESSION MAY 1987
THIRD IMPRESSION AUGUST 1987
FOURTH IMPRESSION MARCH 1988

BOOK, COVER AND SLIP CASE DESIGN BY CARROLL, DEMPSEY & THIRKELL
LIMITED

BRITISH LIBRARY CATALOGUING IN PUBLICATION DATA

POSTGATE, SARAH
PATTERNS FOR PAPERS-(THE VICTORIA AND ALBERT COLOUR BOOKS)
1. PAPER WORK-PATTERN DESIGN
1. TITLE II. SERIES
769 TT870

ISBN 0-86350-148-6

PRODUCTION BY FACER PUBLISHING
COLOUR REPRODUCTION BY PENINSULAR REPRO SERVICE, EXETER
TYPESET IN GREAT BRITAIN BY OPTIC

PRINTED AND BOUND IN HONG KONG BY
MANDARIN OFFSET

THE VICTORIA AND ALBERT COLOUR BOOKS

PATTERNS FOR PAPERS

INTRODUCTION BY
SARAH POSTGATE

WEBB & BOWER
MICHAEL JOSEPH
MCMLXXXVII

 N the 1920s the Curwen Press's strikingly attractive *Pattern Papers* by English artists and designers such as Paul Nash, Lovat Fraser, Albert Rutherston, Edward Bawden and Enid Marx became fashionable among certain publishing, manufacturing and artistic circles. This little book presents a selection of Curwen papers, dating from the early 1920s to the early 1950s, by the lesser-known as well as the famous – all held by the Department of Designs, Prints and Drawings in the Victoria and Albert Museum.

Paul Nash, introducing *A Specimen Book of Pattern Papers designed for and in use at The Curwen Press*, published by The Fleuron in 1928, defined his term 'pattern papers'. These, he suggested, were to be distinguished from traditional decorative papers because they were printed by modern machine methods, not hand-decorated with block-printing, marbling or the paste method, as was done in the past. Decorative and pattern papers' chief functions relate to book design and the bookbinder's craft: to decorate the boards of books, to form loose book covers and to act as endpapers (papers placed at the beginning and end of the book, the outer half pasted to the inside of the boards, the inner forming the fly leaf). Nash mentions more possible uses: lining the insides of boxes and cupboards, acting as wallpaper or making envelopes with card backs for carrying paperwork, a contemporary suggestion. The term 'pattern paper' for a particular type of decorative paper has gained currency, though it is often modified to the less misleading 'patterned paper'.

The Curwen Press was started by the Reverend John Curwen in 1863. His grandson, Harold Curwen, made radical changes which were, in due course, to transform this commercial press into a leading light of the printing revival of the 1920s. Reacting against the general decline in typographical standards, he chose good-quality type, paper and inks, appropriate to the particular piece to be printed.

Claud Lovat Fraser (1890-1921), a young designer whose influential stage designs for *The Beggar's Opera* (1920) brought him fame, played a vital role in the period 1919-21 in establishing Curwen's policy of 'courageous printing'. Lovat Fraser's interests and tastes coincided exactly with his patron's; he was soon producing a whole range of colourful, lighthearted, decorative work for the Press's commercial or 'jobbing' work, all intended 'To Put the Spirit of Joy into Printed Things' (as a publicity leaflet of 1920 urged). It was Lovat Fraser who was, by all accounts, the instigator of the Curwen Press's pattern papers series. Inspired by a blank notebook covered with traditional Florentine patterned covers given to him by Edward Gordon Craig, he produced twenty similar designs, which Curwen bought. This led to more commissions for papers from artists and the idea of publishing a specimen book. The project was started in about 1920 and the book came out in 1928.

Ten designers contributed thirty-one pattern papers to the *Specimen Book*. Seven made drawings and the rest wood-engraved key units, which were then repeated lithographically. The folded sample sheets of strong, firm paper measured 20 ins by 25 ins. The book, with a Paul Nash introduction and pattern paper cover, sold as a limited edition. The 'draughtsmen' were Lovat Fraser, Albert Rutherston, Margaret James, Thomas Lowinsky, E O Hoppé, Edward Bawden, Paul Nash; the 'wood engravers' Nash, Enid Marx, Eric Ravilious and Harry Carter.

Lovat Fraser's invention, versatility and stylish wit are apparent. He ranged from the large scale (similar to that of wallpaper) and showy *(plates 17, 18)*, to the small and delicate; from geometrics to florals. Most artists kept to the formula of a small unit of pattern repeated regularly over the whole sheet, but Lovat Fraser's design of seaweed-like strips of colour is emphatically bold – though in fact readable in all directions as a satisfying pattern should be. His use of bright flowers on dark backgrounds were fashionable during the 1920s in textile design – seen in the work of Percy Bilbie, for instance; in the 1930s, Albert Rutherston took up this idea again *(plates 11, 12)*. Bakst's exotic colours for the Diaghilev ballet had strongly influenced Lovat Fraser and others of his generation. Lovat Fraser may well have drawn these patterns with a broad reed pen and brightly coloured inks, producing a splodgy outline.

Albert Rutherston (1881-1953), trained at the Slade School of Fine Art and was a close friend of Lovat Fraser and much influenced by him. Probably as a reaction to the late arrival in England of the revolutionary developments in European art, which began with Roger Fry's Post-Impressionists exhibition in 1910, Rutherston adopted a linear, decorative style, rejecting illusionism, and turned to specializing in the applied arts. This can be seen in his pen and watercolour work shown here *(plates 5, 6, 7, 11, 12, 15, 25 and 26)*: the small, delicate arabesques and flowers have a nonchalant, faux-naif charm, and his colour combinations – pale blues, pinks, greys and purples – are delightfully subtle.

The post-war Royal College of Art, under the new Principal, William Rothenstein, saw a flowering of the arts: students at that period included Henry Moore, John Tunnard, Eric Ravilious, Edward Bawden, Barnett Freedman and Enid Marx. Several of these went on to work for Curwen, especially in their early years. Already recognized as a war artist, Paul Nash, restlessly trying wood engraving, textile design, writing and teaching, accepted a position as visiting tutor of design.

The introduction of wood-engraved designs for some pattern papers into the *Specimen Book*, starting in 1925 with Paul Nash's 'Crocus' design *(plate 16)*, reflected a contemporary revival of interest in that medium as a means of artistic expression. In 1920 the Society of Wood Engravers was set up by Robert Gibbings and Noel Rooke; Nash was a founder member and later Ravilious and Marx joined. Nash's three wood-engraved *Specimen Book*

papers, executed in 1925-8, show him responding imaginatively and directly to the problems of the medium, often with strong, structured results, rather Art Deco in feeling. Two designs are starkly printed in black on to the white paper *(plate 16)*; in the 'Steps' design he experimented by adding to the black a 'starved' yellow band, lithographically repeated. Nash used a graver for cutting. The design of eclipsed moons (1927 – *plate 2*), for which he did an initial drawing, looks back in style to his pre-war romantic paintings of night skies and falling stars.

Enid Marx, born in 1902, has worked in many fields, including print-making, textile design, book illustration and poster design. At the Royal College of Art, she learnt wood engraving from Ravilious and Harold Curwen gave her her first job. She did several pattern paper designs for Curwen from 1925-35; they show her usual concern for pattern and texture. In her earliest design (1925 – *plate 13*), exploiting the textural variations possible in wood engraving, she has built up a small frame enclosing a central disc. Her white-on-black technique recalls Ravilious and derives from Bewick. The indigo colour belongs to her range of spicy colours which include blues, browns, buff, interspersed with blacks. Other papers are larger in scale and bolder; one is a lino-cut design (1927).

Although Edward Bowden (born 1903) later worked in watercolour, his early commissions (often from Curwen) were mainly for graphic designs. At the post-war Royal College, he revealed his natural talent for book illustration, calligraphy and print-making. He had a steady hand and a sharp, sprightly line, evident in his first pattern paper design (1928 – *plate 29*). A pared-down version of a printer's 'flower', related to those recently revived by Morison and Meynell at the Pelican Press, it is a most satisfying

ornament. He worked on a larger scale in a later (1935) example *(plate 1)* – a modernistic, visually playful device, again successful financially for the Press. Thirties-style colours were chosen – muddy green and brown, and aquamarine. Two versions have a delicate 'litho grain' effect in the background. Both designs were copper-engraved and then, by means of intaglio transfer, lithographically repeated.

By 1934 Barnett Freedman (1901-58) was already established as a book illustrator and designer of posters, advertisements and book jackets. Harold Curwen encouraged him to develop his skill at autolithography, a technique which Curwen pioneered. Autolithography differed from the commercial lithographic process in that the work was printed directly from the artist's original drawings or paintings on to stone, plate or transfer paper; usually the artist's design was copied by a skilled lithographist. The pattern paper here *(plates 19, 20)* is quite an early example of the technique. Because the artist draws with lithographic chalk on to a grained surface, certain attractive effects can result such as gradations of tone, textural variations and soft-edged, clear colours. Overprinted colours play an important role in the design for Freedman seemed fond of this device. He shows his obvious technical mastery and skill in what is perhaps an over-elaborate design, the only autolithographic pattern paper Curwen produced.

Graham Sutherland (1903-80) had met Oliver Simon, a director at the Curwen Press, in about 1935 and later they became friends; this led to a long creative relationship. Sutherland's first attempt at a pattern paper design in 1937 was not particularly successful financially – only thirty-two sheets in all were sold. Shortly afterwards he transformed the simple motif by adding pen and ink shadows and hatching (probably copper-engraved) to the pastilles.

A SPECIMEN BOOK OF
PATTERN PAPERS
DESIGNED FOR AND IN USE AT
THE CURWEN PRESS
WITH AN INTRODUCTION BY PAUL NASH

PUBLISHED FOR THE CURWEN PRESS BY
THE FLEURON LIMITED
101 GREAT RUSSELL STREET LONDON
1928

This was printed in characteristically acrid colour combinations *(plates 31, 32)* – pink on yellow and blue on pink, the artist having indicated the correct shade by sending a scrap of pink card.

Of the female artists whose work is illustrated in this book, except for Enid Marx, there appears to exist little documentary evidence. Margaret James was probably active between 1922 and 1966, and Althea Willoughby in the 1920s to 1930s. Sarah Neckemkin (active 1937-62) worked for Curwen in the late 1930s and probably late 1940s. Her forties' designs *(plates 3, 4, 28)* are colourful and cheery, with perhaps a touch of English folk art; maybe Lovat Fraser influenced her. Elizabeth Friedländer (b.1903) did much cover design work for Penguin Books in the 1950s when Hans Schmoller (1916-85), recently arrived from Curwen, revived the patterned paper style cover (with pasted-on label) for the paperback *Music Scores* and *Poetry* series. Her designs of geometrics, printer's flowers and florals are stylized, precise and small-scale; her colours are bright, almost brash.

The dogged production of a few papers continued into the 1960s, by which time Harold Curwen and Oliver Simon had both died. Sadly, in 1982, the Curwen Press was put into the hands of the liquidators. However, post-war initiatives – the Curwen Prints workshop and Curwen Gallery – flourish. The Press's effects were sold off, and today only some of the original pattern paper range is available, bought up by Falkiner Fine Papers Ltd of Long Acre. Thus this important collection of ephemera, which records the changing twentieth-century English artistic and decorative styles, has become historic and yet, in part at least, continues to survive.

BIBLIOGRAPHY

Harley, B, *The Curwen Press: a Short History*, Curwen Press, 1970.

Peppin, B and Micklethwait, L, *Dictionary of British Book Illustrators: the Twentieth Century*, John Murray, 1983.

Simon, H, *Song and Words: a History of the Curwen Press*, George Allen & Unwin, 1973.

Simon, O, *Printer and Playground*, Faber and Faber, 1956.

Tate Gallery, *Artists at Curwen: a celebration of the gift of artists' prints from the Curwen Studio*, exhibition catalogue by Pat Gilmour, 1977.

Victoria and Albert Museum, *Paul Nash as Designer*, exhibition catalogue by Susan Lambert, 1975.

KEY TO PLATES

All works illustrated probably originated from drawings unless otherwise stated.

E Bawden 29. 1928, 1. 1935 (lithographically repeated from engraved copper plate) B Freedman 19.20. 1934 (autolithographic process) E Friedlander 9.10.23.30 late 1940s M James 14. 1927 C Lovat Fraser 17.18. 1922, 21.24. 1923, 22.1928 E Marx 13. 1925 (lithographically repeated from wood-engraved key unit) P Nash 16. 1925, 2. 1927 (lithographically repeated from wood-engraved unit) S Neckemkin 3.4.28 late 1940s E Ravilious 27. 1927 (lithographically repeated from wood-engraved unit) A Rutherston 7. 1923, 25. 1925, 5. 1926, 6.15. 1927, 26. pre 1928, 11.12. 1934 G Sutherland 31.32. 1937 A Willoughby 8. 1929 (lithographically repeated from wood-engraved unit)

The author would like to thank the following for permission to reproduce illustrations: E Bawden *pls 1,29*; Mrs C Freedman *pls 19,20*; E Marx *pl 13*, Paul Nash Trust *pls 2,16*; J. Ravilious *pl 27*; the Rutherston family *pls 5,6,7,12,15,25,26*; Mr M Willoughby *pl 8*; © ADAGP, Paris and CosmoPress, Geneva, 1986, *pl 31,32*.

THE PLATES

1

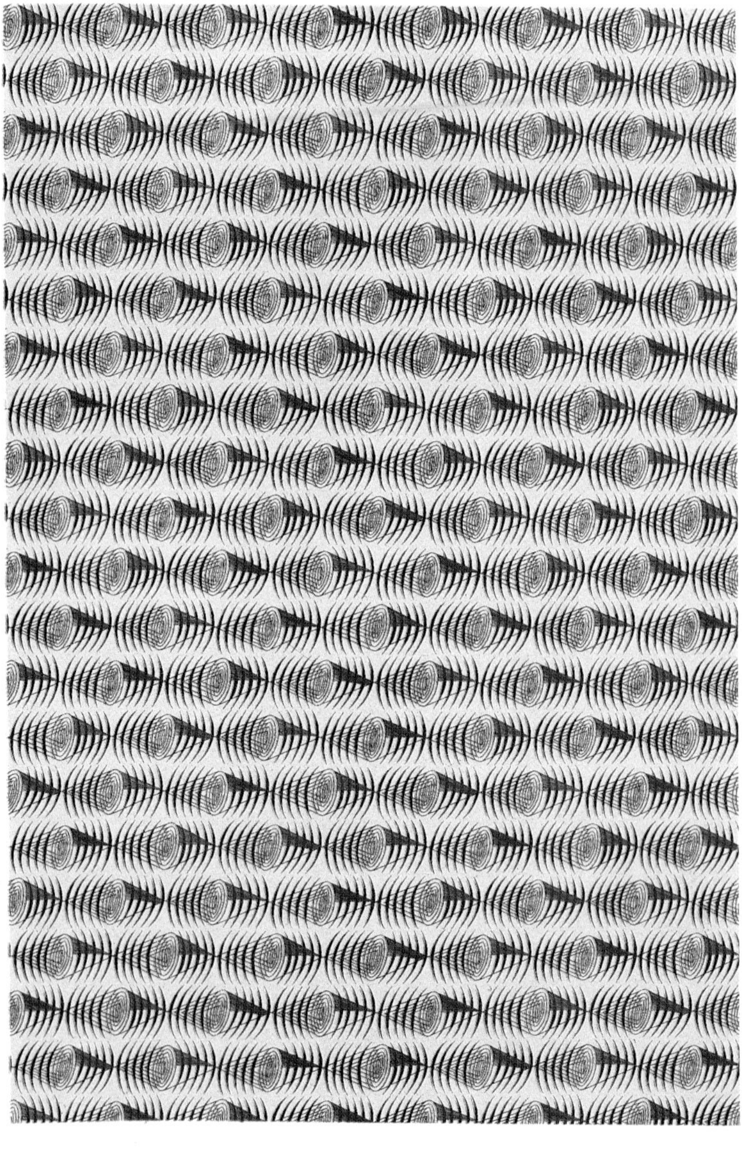

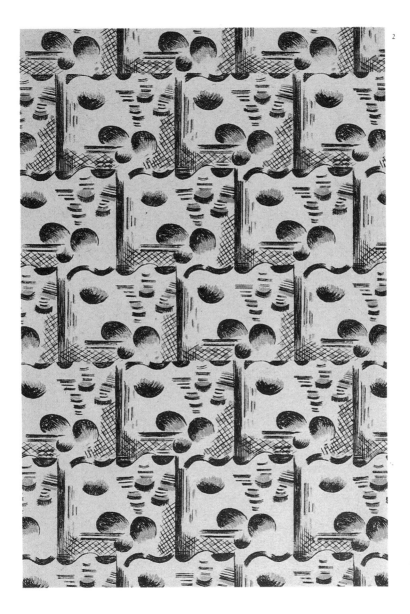

2

3

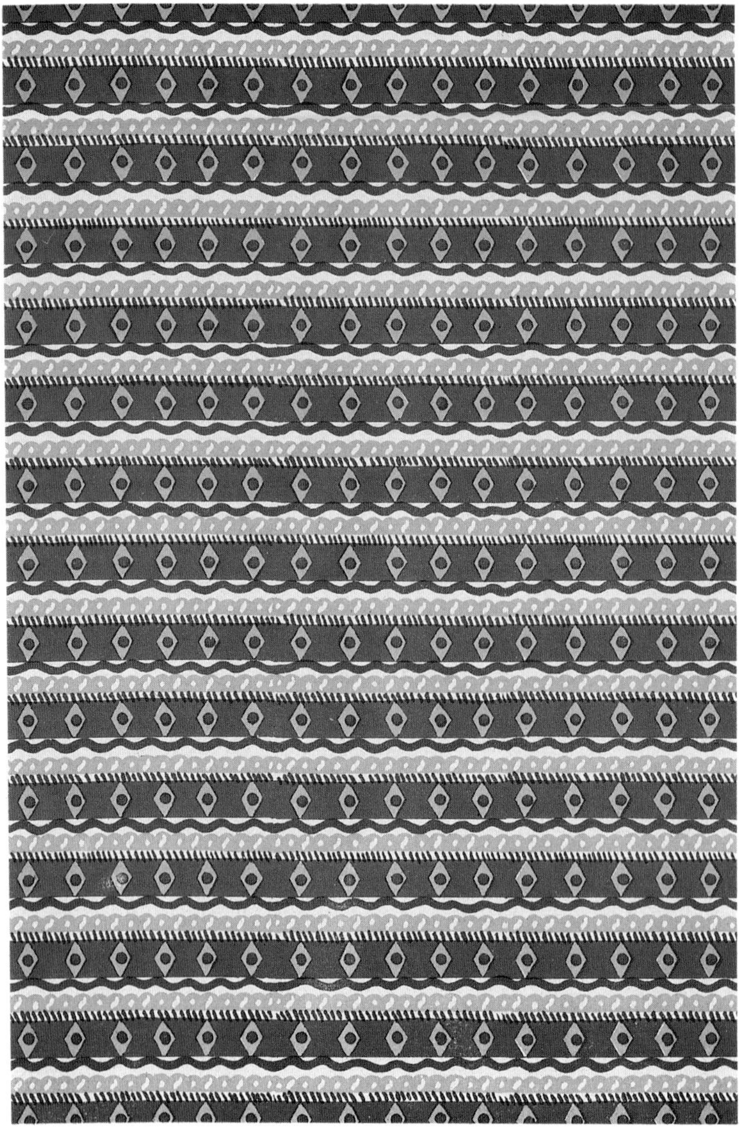

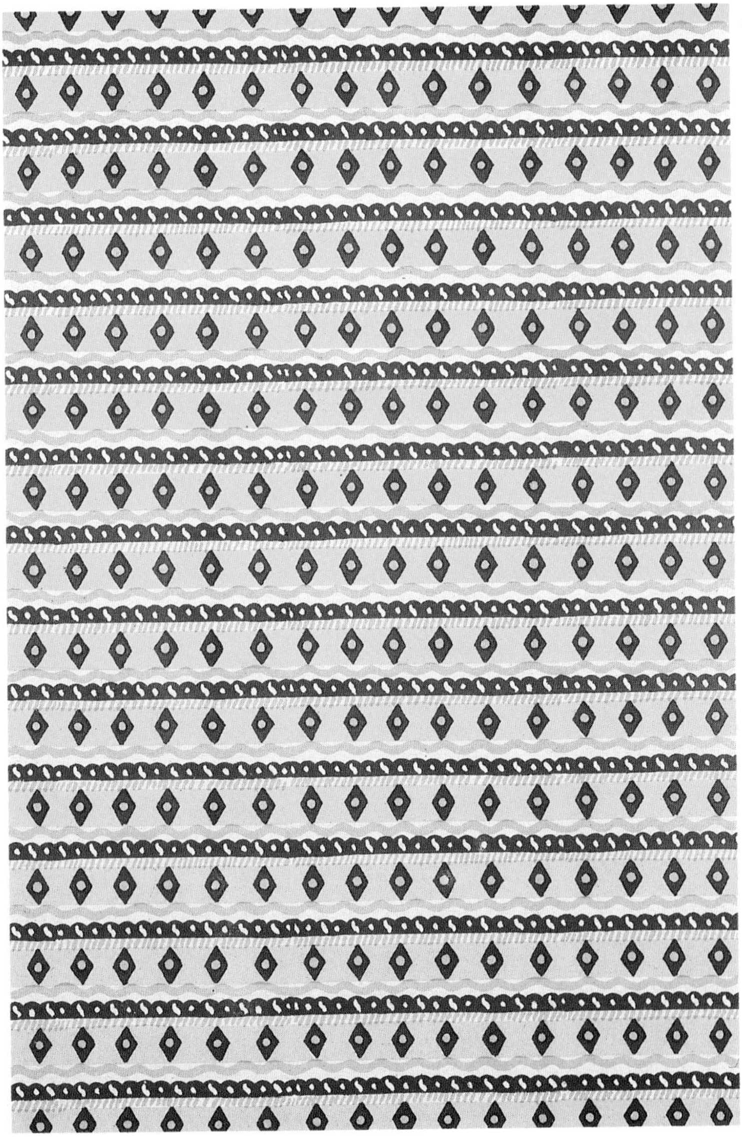

4

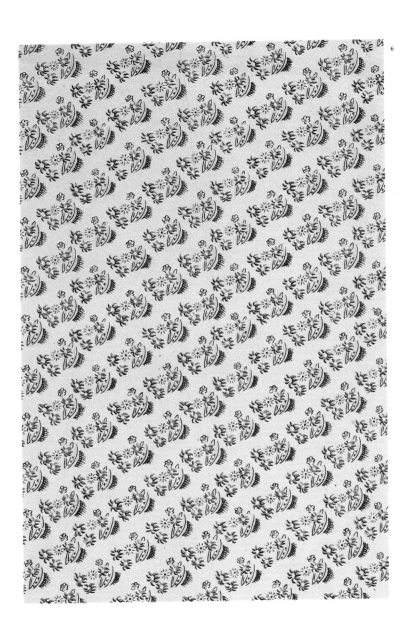

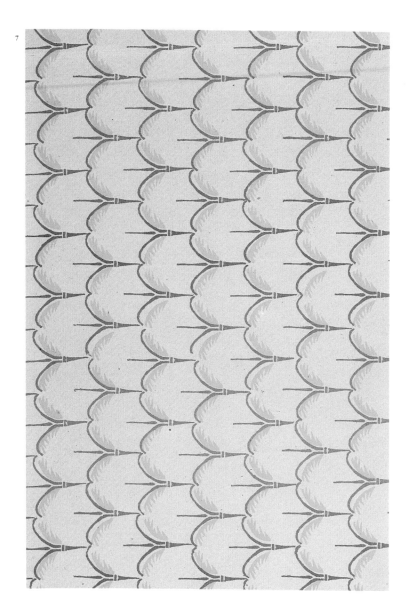

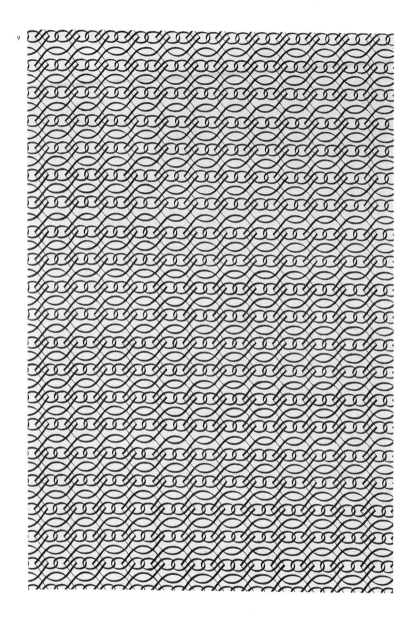

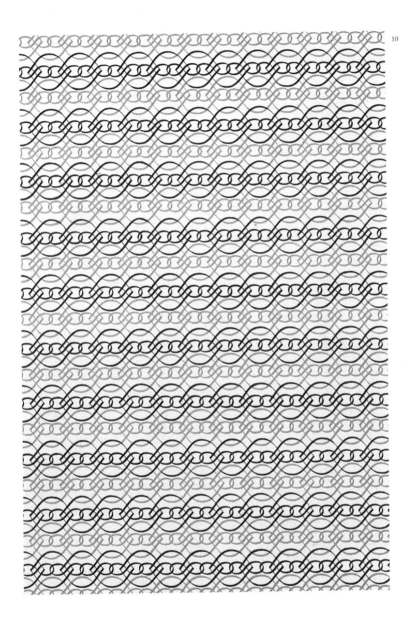

11

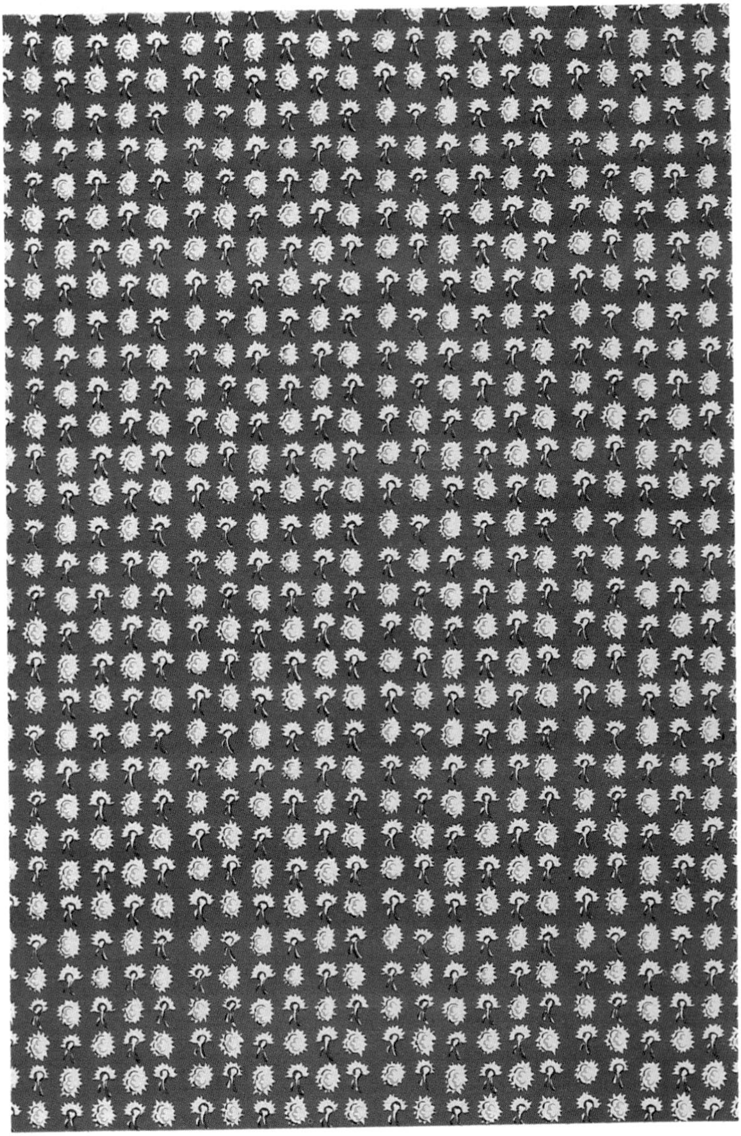

12

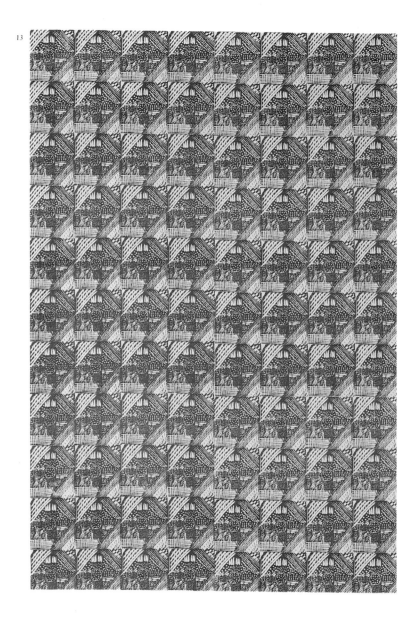

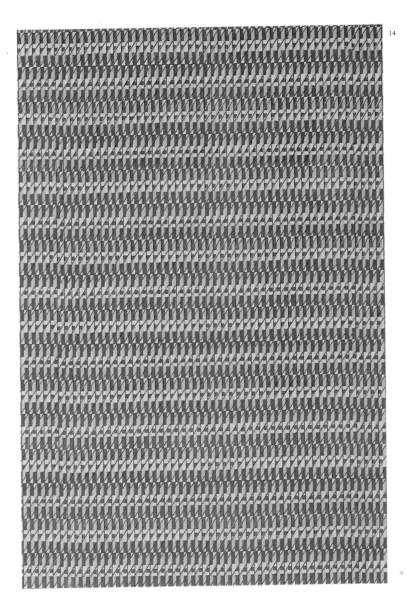

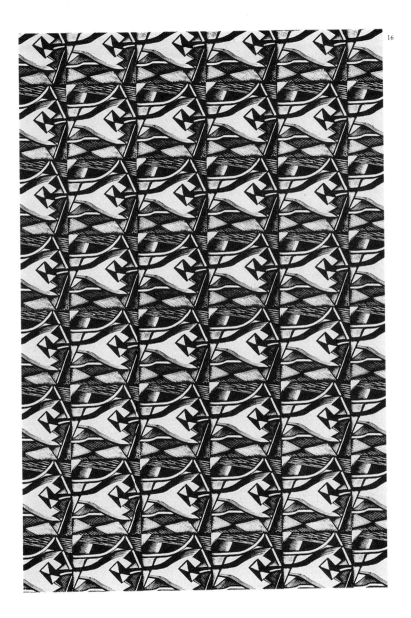

17

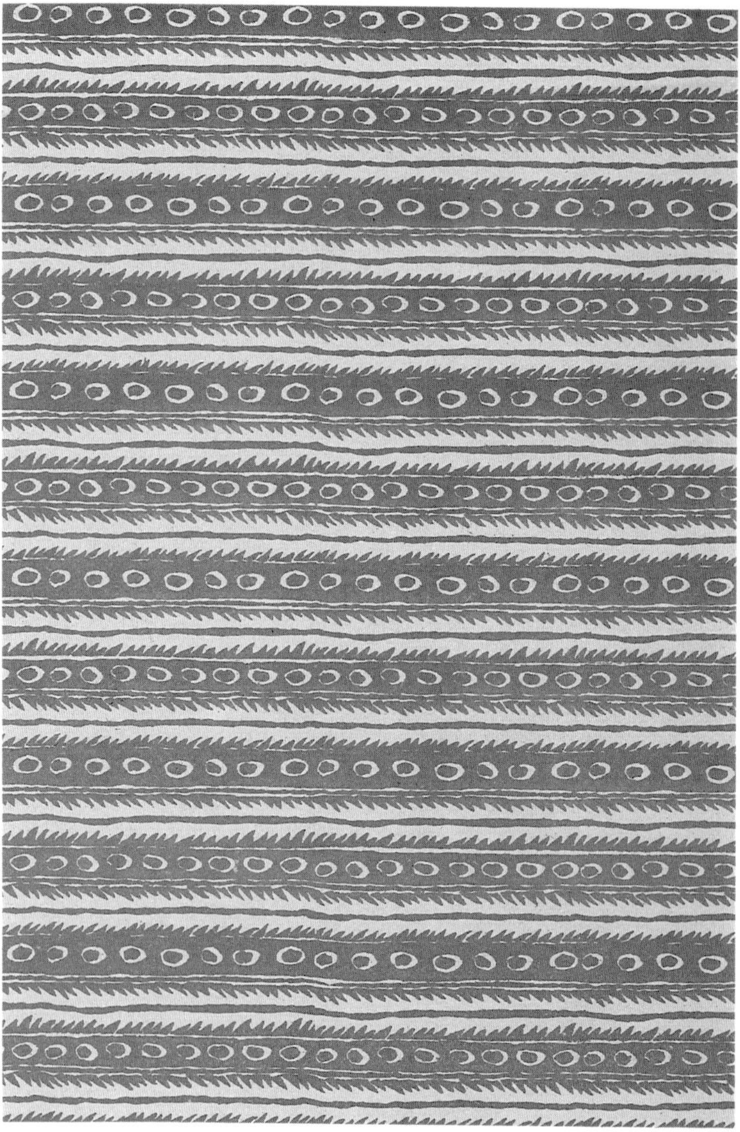

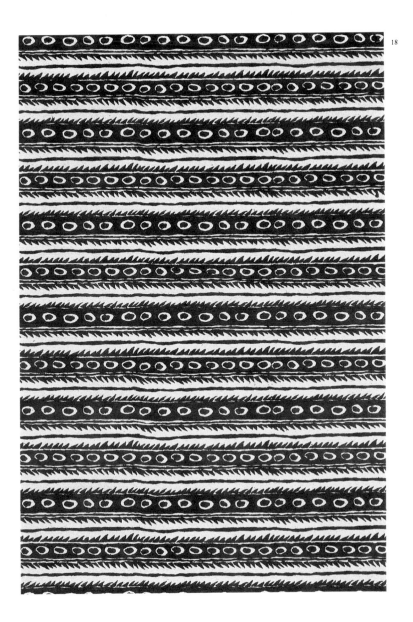

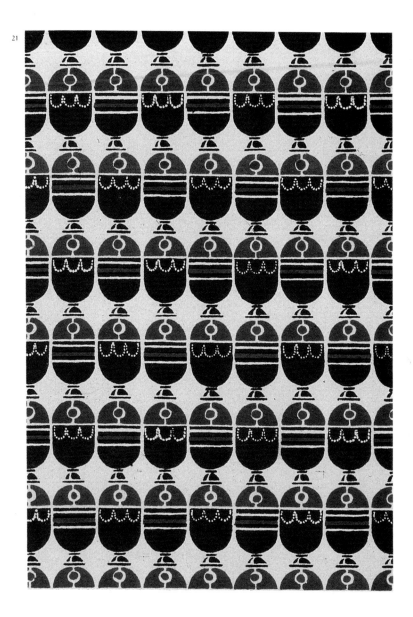

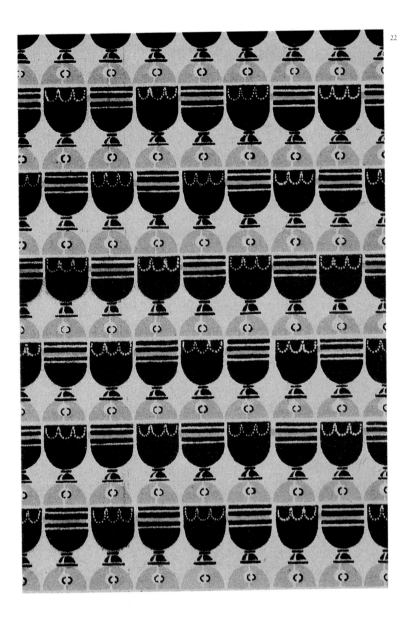

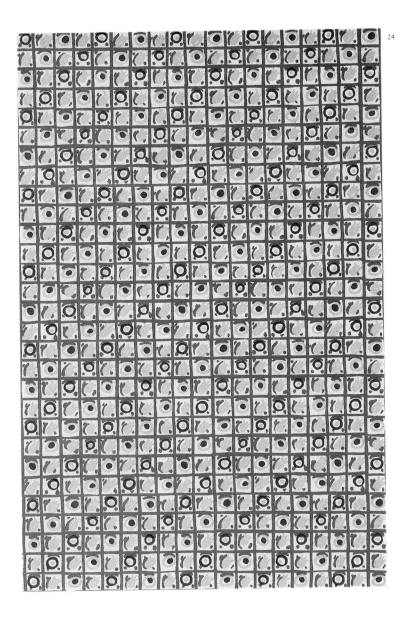

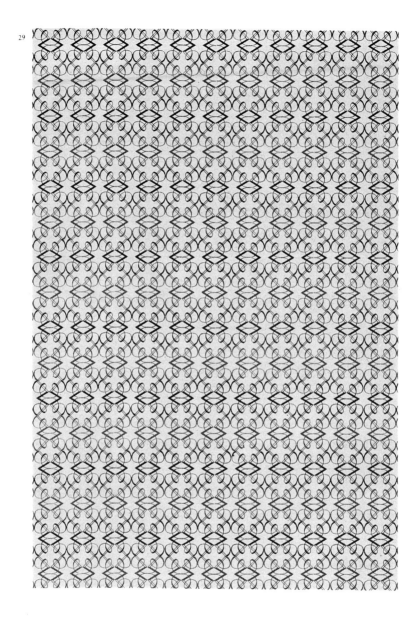

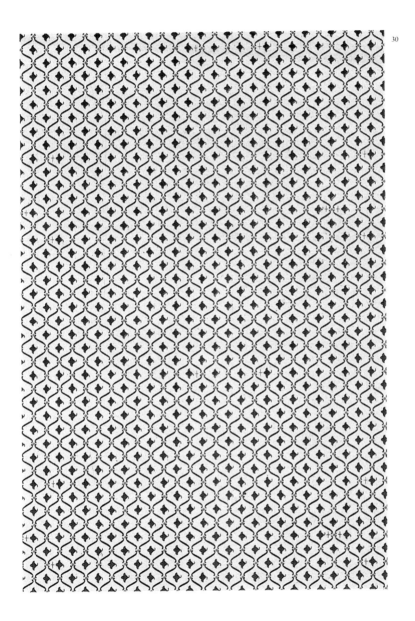

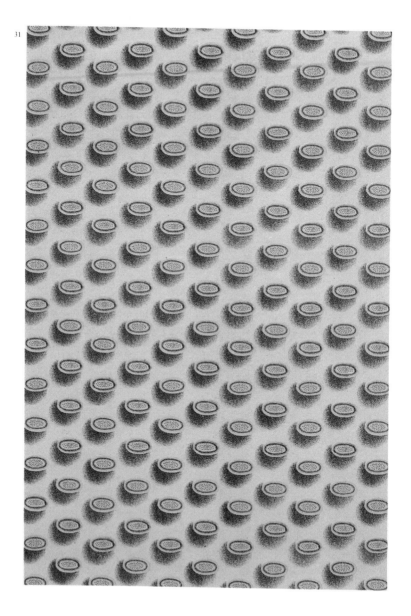

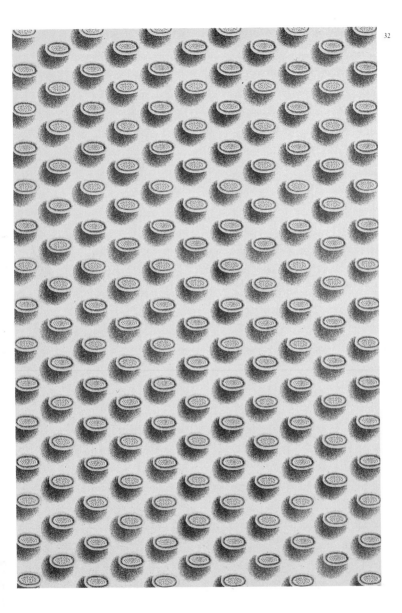